# TITLE I MATERIALS

Georgetown Elementary School
Indian Prairie School District
Aurora, Illinois

# Waterfalls

by Mari Schuh

**Consulting Editor:** Gail Saunders-Smith, PhD

**Consultant:** Nikki Strong, PhD
St. Anthony Falls Laboratory
University of Minnesota

**CAPSTONE PRESS**
a capstone imprint

Pebble Plus is published by Capstone Press,
151 Good Counsel Drive, P.O. Box 669, Mankato, Minnesota 56002.
www.capstonepub.com

032010
005740CGF10

*Library of Congress Cataloging-in-Publication Data*
Schuh, Mari C., 1975–
    Waterfalls / by Mari Schuh.
    p. cm.—(Pebble plus. Natural wonders)
    Includes bibliographical references and index.
    Summary: "Simple text and full-color photos explain how waterfalls form and why they are an important landform"—Provided by publisher.
    ISBN 978-1-4296-5002-1 (library binding)
    ISBN 978-1-4296-5586-6 (paperback)
    1. Waterfalls—Juvenile literature. I. Title. II. Series.
GB1403.8.S88 2011
551.48'4—dc22                                                              2010002794

**Editorial Credits**
Katy Kudela, editor; Heidi Thompson, designer; Kelly Garvin, media researcher; Eric Manske, production specialist

**Photo Credits**
Dreamstime/Chanyut Sribua-rawd, 9; Hazel Brown, 5; Jason Yoder, 7; Olga Khoroshunova, cover
Fotolia/Sascha F., 1
Getty Images Inc./National Geographic/Annie Griffiths Belt, 13; Tom Till, 21
The Granger Collection, New York, 15
Shutterstock/ArnaudS2, 11; Conny Sjostrom, 17; Galyna Andrushko, 19

## Note to Parents and Teachers

The Natural Wonders series supports national geography standards related to the physical and human characteristics of places. This book describes and illustrates waterfalls. The images support early readers in understanding the text. The repetition of words and phrases helps early readers learn new words. This book also introduces early readers to subject-specific vocabulary words, which are defined in the Glossary section. Early readers may need assistance to read some words and to use the Table of Contents, Glossary, Read More, Internet Sites, and Index sections of the book.

# Table of Contents

# How a Waterfall Forms

A river slowly wears away

its rocky bed.

A steep cliff forms.

The rushing water plunges

to the rocks below.

Waterfalls form when water
flows from a high place
to a low place.
Most waterfalls form
in the mountains.

# Kinds of Waterfalls

There are different kinds

of waterfalls.

Cascades flow over

rocky steps.

Cataracts are large
and powerful.
These waterfalls drop
in long streams
from high cliffs.

Every waterfall has

its own shape and size.

Victoria Falls in Africa stretches

1 mile (1.6 kilometers) wide.

# Making Power

Long ago, people used waterfalls to power mills. Moving water powered wheels and machines inside the mills.

15

Today, waterfalls are
still a source of power.
People use waterfalls
to make electricity.

# Famous Waterfalls

Each year, millions of people

visit Niagara Falls.

These two huge waterfalls

are found between Canada

and the United States.

19

Angel Falls is the world's

tallest waterfall.

Found in Venezuela,

it is 3,212 feet

(979 meters) tall.

# Glossary

bed—the bottom of a body of water

cliff—a high, steep rock face; cliffs are found on the sides of hills and mountains

electricity—a form of energy used to power lights and other machines

mill—a factory; people used waterfalls to power flour, lumber, and other kinds of mills

plunge—to fall steeply or sharply

# Read More

Rau, Dana Meachen. *Waterfalls*. Bookworms: Wonders of Nature. New York: Marshall Cavendish Benchmark, 2008.

Watson, Galadriel Findlay. *Angel Falls: The Highest Waterfall in the World*. Natural Wonders. New York: Weigl, 2005.

# Internet Sites

FactHound offers a safe, fun way to find Internet sites related to this book. All of the sites on FactHound have been researched by our staff.

Here's all you do:

*Visit www.facthound.com*

FactHound will fetch the best sites for you!

# Index

Word Count: 150
Grade: 1
Early-Intervention Level: 19